# MAGIC
## Its Ritual, Power and Purpose

A classic introduction to the theory and
practice of magic in which the aim of the genuine
magician is seen to be the realisation of that True Self
of which the earthly personality is but the mask.

*By the same author*

AN INTRODUCTION TO TELEPATHY
APPRENTICED TO MAGIC
HOW TO DEVELOP CLAIRVOYANCE
HOW TO DEVELOP PSYCHOMETRY
HOW TO READ THE AURA
MAGIC AND THE QABALAH
THE MAGICIAN: HIS TRAINING AND WORK

# MAGIC
## Its Ritual, Power and Purpose

*By*
W.E. BUTLER

THOTH PUBLICATIONS
Loughborough, Leicestershire

A CIP catalogue record for this book is available from the
British Library.

ISBN 978 1913660116

Published by
Thoth Publications
64, Leopold Street, Loughborough, LE11 5DN
web address: www.thoth.co.uk
e-mail: enquiries@thoth.co.uk

# CONTENTS

IT is obviously impossible to fully cover such a vast subject as Magic in the small compass of these pages. 1 have therefore attempted to give a general idea of one aspect of the Magical Art in the hope that this little book may encourage my readers in the serious study of the Science of the Magi.

Acknowledgements are due to my wife, for her help and encouragement, and to Bishop Robert King of the Liberal Catholic Church and the late Dion Fortune, Founder and first Warden of the Fraternity of the Inner Light, for the teaching and advice I have received from them. It is fair to add that none of them are to be held responsible for the ideas herein expressed.

W. E. BUTLER.

February 16th, 1952.

# CHAPTER 1

## SOME DEFINITIONS AND A GENERAL SURVEY

IN this imperfect world, where it is so easy to misunderstand or to be misunderstood, it is necessary, when writing upon such a subject as ceremonial magic, to define carefully one's terms. But before giving any definition, let us deal with the popularly accepted ideas of magic. By so doing we may cut away much of the obscuring undergrowth of thought, as one might clear away the tropical vegetation from around some hidden Aztec temple, and so reveal its true proportions and appearance.

The simile is apposite, for the temple of magic has been so overgrown with the lush growth of uninformed and superstitious thought throughout the ages that, in the Western world at least, its true appearance and nature has been lost. Only amongst the ignorant and superstitious on the one hand, and a certain nucleus of informed and instructed magicians on the other, has any idea of the true nature of magic been retained, and in the former case that idea has been sadly distorted and bears very little relationship to the actual facts.

As students of archaeology and the learned exponents of comparative religion alike inform us, magic goes back to the very beginnings of human life on this planet. All systems of religion, with the exception, possibly of certain Protestant sects and the Southern Buddhists, have at some period or other in their history made use of ceremonial magic. Those who are interested in the historical aspect of the subject will find listed in the bibliography at the end of this book works by recognised experts in the field, foremost among them being Sir James Frazer, whose *Golden Bough* is a classic.

If these authorities were carefully studied, it will be observed that broadly speaking, each succeeding religion assimilates the best in the religion it supersedes, and the remainder is left to the ignorant populace and to those priests of the old religion who will not conform to the new. As the new religion organises itself it begins to persecute the remnant of the old, and this remnant is driven underground.

Such a state of affairs arose when Christianity emerged from its infancy and became the dominant religion of the West. The old religion disintegrated and the Christian Church absorbed much of its philosophy and ritual, gradually permeating all levels of society, until the only followers of the old faith were the rustics, the dwellers in outlying and isolated places. These rustics or *pagani*, untrained in the philosophy of their religion, handed down a distorted semblance of it. Always in the background, they were often cruelly persecuted, but their numbers were constantly recruited from many sources, including those who rebelled against the Papal claims.

When, however, the impulse of the Renaissance began to make it possible to break the yoke of Rome, the very godly Reformed Churches were as bitter as Rome had been in their persecution of the witches, wizards and magicians. The history of Europe from the XIth to the XVIIIth century makes harrowing reading. With the emergence of the "Age of Reason" popular belief in the malign power of the magician began to disappear. Concurrently, in Protestant circles at least, religious belief began to deteriorate into a formality that had very little driving force.

This dead level of mediocrity in England reached its high water mark in Victorian days, when physical science in the form of one of its greatest exponents declared "there is no room in the universe for ghosts," and the President of the Royal Society said, "In matter I see the promise and potency of all life." But with the increasing knowledge of the universe which modern developments in science have brought, such ideas have had to be considerably revised, and the modern physicist such as Jeans, Eddington or Einstein, has propounded an idea of the nature and purpose of the universe which can readily be accepted by the magician. Allowing for the difference in terminology, he has been saying the same thing for centuries past!

It is, however, with the modern school of psychology, more particularly that presentation of it which is associated with the name of C. G. Jung that the magician finds his closest link with modern thought. By that curious swing of the mental pendulum, first noted by Heraclitus, termed *enantiodromia*, that which has been repressed and driven underground now begins to flourish in the open, to the manifest dismay of the orthodox communions.

But although repressed and persecuted throughout the ages, magic never ceased to exist in the Western world. The Roman Church had skilfully adapted much of the old magic to subserve her own purposes, but behind the scenes the magical tradition ran like one of the underground rivers of the Peak district, emerging now and then into the light of day, and then disappearing again beneath the surface.

One such emergence was the Order of the Temple, whose members, the Knights Templar have been cleared of much of the odium cast upon them by their persecutors; the Albigenses in France were another; the Brethren of the Golden and Rosy Cross, the Illuminati, the Magnetists, the Theosophists and the numerous magical Orders and Fraternities which appeared in the latter half of the XIXth century were others. Of these, the most famous and the most illuminating from our point of view is the "Order of the Golden Dawn." Founded upon an alleged Rosicrucian foundation, it brought into one magnificent synthesis all the floating magical threads and, in spite of many vicissitudes and divisions, it still remains the fountainhead of the Western magical tradition.

So much for our general survey of the magical field. Now for our definitions.

My dictionary gives me the popular definition of magic – "The art of applying natural causes to produce surprising results." Such a definition covers too much ground. It could be applied by a savage to the radio, the telephone or the aeroplane, though such a one would probably conclude that supernatural, not natural causes were at work! A modern magician who has written extensively upon the subject has defined magic as "the art of causing changes at will." Again, this is too wide a definition – it would include the operations of all workers, both manual and mental, who certainly produce changes at will.

In the present writers' opinion, the best definition of magic is that given by another modern magician who has defined it as "the art of causing changes in consciousness at will." This agrees with both the theory and practice of magic and we may profitably employ it here, with due acknowledgements to its originator. "Dion Fortune," who was amongst other things, the Warden of a well-organised magical fraternity.

Having arrived at a suitable definition, we are confronted with another difficulty. What do we mean by "changes in consciousness?" It will be necessary, then, for us to consider (a) what is consciousness, and (b) what is meant by changes in it. In the next chapter we will consider the modern psychological view of human personality. It must be remembered, however, that psychology is not yet sufficiently developed, as a science, to be hailed as a unified body of knowledge.

There are several schools of psychology, differing in their explanations of the observed facts. The followers of Freud place the greatest emphasis upon one aspect of life, the followers of

Jung upon another, the pupils of Adler upon yet another. It will be seen that the bias of the present writer is in the direction of the Jungian school.

As a matter of fact, the writings of C. G. Jung are so much in line with the magical tradition that it is easy for us to understand the feeling of some of his more materialistic colleagues that he has "fallen away into mysticism." The results of this falling away seem to be satisfactory from the psychotherapeutic point of view, anyway, and it is the considered opinion of the present writer that in Jung we have the Darwin of the New Psychology. One is aware that this is not an original opinion – others have said the same – but it bears repeating.

# CHAPTER 2

## HUMAN PERSONALITY

THE problem of human personality is one that has remained unsolved for many centuries in the Western world. Eastern thought has evolved a classification of human personality which throws much light upon man's mental processes, but in the West dogmatic theology has up to recent times, limited any similar development of Occidental thought on the subject.

Within recent years, however, many factors over which dogmatic religion has no control have conspired together to put forward a truer view of the real nature of the personality than that hitherto held. The old academic psychology dealt purely with the waking consciousness, and its method of research was mainly by the conscious inturning of the mind upon itself. But many facts began to emerge which pointed to the possibility that the mind of man was greater than was realised. The observed phenomena of mesmerism and hypnotism, telepathy and the psychic marvels of the spiritualists, all began to show the necessity for a new psychology, based this time upon a much broader foundation than its academic predecessor.

F.W.H.Myers, in his epoch-making book *Human Personality*, roughed out the general theory of what he termed the "subliminal mind." The general idea (which still remains valid) was that the conscious mind was that part of the mind that was above a certain level of consciousness which was known as the *limen* or *threshold*. This supra-liminal or above-threshold consciousness is not, however, the only level of consciousness. Below the threshold there exist other layers of consciousness, and these are termed the subliminal levels, or, generally, the 'subconscious.'

So the mind of man, according to this hypothesis is dual, having a conscious or waking level, and a subconscious, which remains below the threshold. Myers showed that all the various phenomena he was considering could be explained on the assumption that under certain conditions and through certain channels, the subconscious could thrust itself up and emerge into the waking life. He showed, too, that this subconscious level of the mind was much greater in its extent and potentialities than the conscious levels of the personality.

The simile, which is usually employed, is that of the iceberg, the greater part of which is hidden in the ocean. Such a simile is an excellent one, since the behaviour of such a berg closely parallels the behaviour of the mind, It often happens, for instance, that although the wind may be blowing from one point of the compass, the berg will move majestically against it, since its great submerged bulk is actuated by ocean currents far below the surface. So it is with the mind of man.

Upon this new concept a new psychology began to be built, and two men stand out as pioneers in the field. The first name is that of Sigmund Freud, and the second is that of his pupil, C.G. Jung. Freudian psychology is familiar to the general public because of its insistence upon the sexual element in psychological disease. With this extreme view, Jung disagreed, and gradually formed what is known as the "Zurich School." From the magical point of view, there can be no doubt that Jung's teachings are closer to the facts than those of Freud, and it is certain aspects of his system, therefore, which I will now briefly outline.

It is understood that behind the manifest life of both animals and humanity there is a driving force or energy that has been given many names. The psychologists refer it to as the *libido* or sometimes the *Id*. This basic urge manifests itself in what are termed the fundamental instincts, and in the usual classification these are held to be three in number, namely the Self-Preservation Instinct or Will-to-Live; the Sex Instinct, or Will-to-Create; the Herd Instinct or Social Urge.

To these three, Jung adds a fourth instinct which he claims as the prerogative of man alone, the Religious Instinct. This instinct is a counterpole to the three biological drives of the primitive instincts and is therefore an essential part of the constitution of man. Whatever system of psychology is built up, if it lack this essential point, will fail to cover fully the field of human personality.

Now in the early evolution of man, the three great instincts predominated though even then the religious instinct was definitely at work. As mankind began to advance, the gradually developing conscious mind began to cut down the intensity of some of the instinctive drives, and to divert their energies into new channels. But this was done in an unregulated and ignorant way, so that considerable friction occurred within man's mind.

With the appearance of Christianity, and the fierce reaction it evoked towards the degeneracy of the old faiths, this repression of the natural instincts became intensified and gradually became accepted as part of the Christian Faith itself until, in the Victorian period, it reached its culminating point. The conscious mind, it was affirmed, conforming to a certain ethical code, was the highest achievement of human evolution.

But this has resulted in the gradual increase of what is, in the main, a disease of the Western world, "psycho-neurosis." There are, of course, neurotics in all races, but by far the greater number are to be found in the Western civilisations. The powerful instincts being thrown back upon themselves become twisted and perverted and the energy they should bring to the workings of the conscious mind, were they properly directed, or "sublimated," is lost in internal mental friction, giving rise to that sense of frustration so common in the West.

This repression of the dynamic power of the individual has resulted in the establishment of a hard line of cleavage between the subconscious and the conscious levels of the mind. But it is obvious that only by bringing through into the conscious mind the dynamic power trapped below the threshold can the activities of man reach their true level. It is such a release of the subconscious that is aimed at in modern psychotherapy, and this also is what is attempted in modern magic.

This does not mean that the primitive instincts have to be given full play in their crudest forms, but rather that the driving energy of such instincts is canalised and redirected into other channels. There must be, however, a natural similarity between the energy being redirected or "sublimated" and the new channel of expression that is offered it. An instance of this is the advice given so often to adolescents troubled with excessive sexual urges. They used to be told "Go in for sports, gymnastics, etc., and work it off." Sometimes the remedy succeeded – more often it failed – having apparently increased the urge rather than decreased it. This was because a channel for the first biological drive had been used for a force belonging to the second drive.

Sports are a splendid way of subliminating the Self Preservation Instinct, and such group associations also form a good channel for the Herd Instinct, but they are unsuitable for the Sex Instinct, which is essentially individual and creative. Nowadays the general advice to such sufferers is to engage in the creative arts and crafts, to create, to make, even though it is only a rustic seat in their own garden. Such creative work affords an excellent channel of sublimation.

It must not be thought that the entire energy of such instincts energies should be available for the continued development of the spirit of man. It is here that the fourth instinct posited by Jung comes in, for it is the counterpole drawing the developing man up to greater heights and we might with advantage equate this fourth drive with what the occultists call the Superconscious or Higher Self, and the magician calls the Holy Guardian Angel.

Modern psycho-analytical research has pointed to the existence in the Unconscious or Subconscious of certain levels or layers of development, and the deeper of these levels link the individual not only with the minds of his immediate neighbours, but successively with the mental processes of all mankind down to a certain level, and below that again with the consciousness of the animal and vegetable kingdoms. It would seem that just as our physical bodies bear within their very structure the marks of their evolutionary development from the lower kingdoms of Nature, so our minds show a similar line of ascent.

There is what is termed the "personal subconscious" consisting of ideas, emotions and memories, some of which have been thrust down below the threshold because we refused to acknowledge even to ourselves, that we were capable of such thoughts. Such groups of thought charged with emotional energy are known as "complexes" or "constellations." and where they have been refused acknowledgement they tend to break away from the general unity of the mind and become semi-independent. They are then said to be "dissociated," and it is these dissociated complexes which result in the locking up of the psychic energy of the self. The repressed complexes and the dissociated complexes, together with all the host of forgotten experience, memories and emotions make up this "personal subconscious."

Deeper than this level we come to those emotions and thoughts, those primordial images which we share with all humanity, not only present humanity but past humanity as well. This "collective unconscious" is as it were, the conditioning background of our subconscious mind and the images and memories buried in its depths exercise an influence upon our lives which, though unknown to the waking self, is exceedingly potent.

It is known that the Unconscious, whether personal or collective works by means of pictures or images, speech being a comparatively recent development. Therefore, says Jung:

> Who speaks in primordial images speaks as with a thousand tongues: he grips and overpowers, and at the same time he elevates that which he treats out of the individual and personal transitory into the sphere of the eternal, he exalts the personal lot to the lot of Man and therewith he releases in US too, all those helpful forces which have ever enabled humanity to rescue itself from whatever distress and to live through the longest night.

Magic, with its roots in the immemorial past, does just this, it speaks to the subconscious mind of man through the archaic images of its symbols and rituals, and thereby produces those "changes in consciousness" which the magician seeks. So also it is recorded of the Lord Jesus that "without a parable spake He not unto them." (Mark iv, 34). It was as a Master-Psychologist that He added two positive affirmations that summed up the Mosaic Law.

We may sum up all that has been said in this chapter by saying that the best modern psychological school establishes the existence of four levels of the mind, namely

    (i)      The Conscious Waking Mind.

    (ii)     The Personal Subconsciousness.

    (iii)    The Collective Subconsciousness.

    (iv)    The Superconsciousness.

All these are aspects of the one mind, but of this totality we are normally only aware of one, the waking mind. Nevertheless all the rest constantly affect us so that often we find that the hidden and mysterious currents of the deeper Self impel us along ways we have not consciously chosen.

To be able consciously to become aware of the set of the hidden currents, and turn them to the task of directing our life into the ways of wisdom and the paths of peace is the fervent desire of the magician, who, looking into the depths of his being and seeing therein the spark of eternal light which is his own true centre, exclaims in the name and power of that spark, "I have Omnipotence at my command and Eternity at my disposal."

# CHAPTER 3

## THE MAGICAL THESIS

L EAVING aside all the multitudinous details which surround the subject, we will devote this chapter to a consideration of the magical theory of man and the universe. The magical tradition affirms that the universe is one, and that no part of that universe is *in esse* separate from any other part. As the poet writes, "All are but parts of one stupendous Whole." All that exists in the universe, therefore, is the expression of an underlying unity that subsists through all things. This may be condemned as mere "pantheism" but it is not so in reality, for behind the subsisting unity which expresses itself in the existing universe there is *That* of which the Universal Soul, the Collective Host of Life and Form is but an expression. "Having created the Universe with a Fragment of Myself, I remain," says Deity in the Hindu Scripture, the Bhagavad Gita. A God immanent yet also transcendent is the God of the magician.

The transcendental One, according to the magical teaching is reflected in the Waters of Chaos and Old Night, and that reflection of the Supreme, known as the Adam Kadmon brings order out of chaos. As one magical ritual describes it: " In the Beginning was Chaos and Darkness and the Gates of the Land of Night. And Chaos cried aloud for Unity. Then the Eternal arose. Before the Brightness of that Countenance, the Darkness rolled back, and the Shadows fled away." Now this indwelling reflection, the Adam Kadmon or Great Man of the Kabalah is

the Logos "By Whom all things were made," the Brightness
of His glory and the express Image of His person. Therefore,
nothing in this universe exists except as an integral part of
the Logos. All things subsist in that underlying unity, even as
the Greek poet quoted by St.Paul affirms – "for we also are
His offspring."

The soul of man is part of the greater universe and in
himself is a replica of it. So it is said in Magic that man is
the Microcosm in the Macrocosm, the little universe in the
greater universe. To the magician there is no such thing as
"dead" matter in the Victorian sense. Indeed, he holds the view
that it is only because it already subsists as part of the eternal
life, that anything material can exist in time and space. That
which we see "down here" as an inert block of metal is to
the magician simply the material appearance of innumerable
whirling centres of power, reaching back through the planes
of the invisible worlds to the living heart of all. "The Spirit of
the Lord filleth the Earth," and to the true magician nothing is
common or unclean, for all subserve the purpose and are the
expressions of the life of the eternal. This is declared in the
ritual by the initiated adept who cries: "There is no part of me
that is not a part of the Gods."

"The Gods." Does the magician believe in many gods? Yes,
but his views on their nature are not quite what may be expected
from him. He finds in the universe, visible and invisible, a
mighty field in which innumerable forces play, each force being
an aspect of the Supreme. And in these dancing and scintillant
energies he sees units of the One Life, Sons of God evolved
in previous universes, who as perfect channels of the supreme
power act as living lenses through whom that power is brought
down into manifestation. They are the "Dyan Chohans" of
Eastern Scriptures, the "Ministers, Flames of Fire" of the Bible,
and that Ray of Their essential being which flows from the
unity and is refocused in time and space is the "substance" in
the theological sense which is the "real" universe and which

manifests the secondary qualities that we call matter - the "accidents" of theology.

Thus, in the magical philosophy, there is no dichotomy between spirit and matter; there is no such thing as "dead" matter *per se*. All material existence, all manifestation is but the expression of the all-pervading Life – indeed, it *is that Life* in one of its innumerable modes of being. Believing thus in the life-structure of the universe, the magician holds that just as the power of the unity is manifest through those His ministers, so in the descending or densifying modes of His self-expression, innumerable hosts of lesser intelligences carry out His plan – "Angels and Archangels, Thrones, Dominations, Princedoms, Virtues, Powers; Cherubim and Seraphim, Ashim and all the Ageless Hosts of Heaven" – each in his degree.

The magician, seeing how the Supreme has "constituted the services of angels and men in a wondrous order" sees himself not as a stranger in the universe, not even as a separate being apart from it, but as part of that living diversity in unity, and says with the Greek initiate of old, "I am a Child of Earth, but my Race is from the Starry Heavens."

Turning from the vision of the Heavenly Places, he sees himself in Malkuth, the Kingdom of Earth, and realises that this imperfect, frustrated existence in the physical body, *is* imperfect and frustrated because, although he may know by the intellect of the realities behind the appearances, he has not yet been able to *realise* this truth in the physical world. "Know ye not that ye are gods," says the Christian Scripture, and a modern poet has sung. "Know this, O man, sole root of fault in thee, is not to know thine own divinity."

Over the Temple of the Oracle in ancient days was carved this inscription – *Gnothi Se Auton* – "Know Thyself." It is the realisation of the true nature of the Self that is the aim of the true magician. Following this principle and gazing within himself, the magician beholds a fallen world. He sees that the primal plan upon which man is formed is there, shining through the whole universe as the Supreme Harmony and Beauty, and in this light he sees the ideal in which his personal self is rooted and by which it is sustained.

Then, looking outwards, he sees in his own nature and in the natures of those around him the evidence of a Fall from the Potential Perfection. But in the midst of this Fall he sees the evidence of a Return, and through the sufferings of myriad lives he realises that the Way of Salvation is the Way of Sacrifice.

So he formulates the old Hermetic axiom *Solve et coagula,* which may be rendered as "Dissolve and re-form," and so he uses the rites of the High Magic to effect both that dissolution and that reformation.

But what is dissolved, and what is reformed? Not that Eternal Spark which "lighteth every man" – rather it is the personal self which he has for so long regarded as his only real self, this personality which he has so tenaciously clung to and defended, has pampered and indulged – it is this *persona* this mask of the real man which must be dissolved and reformed. But how shall that which is itself imperfect produce perfection? "Nature unaided, fails," said the old alchemists, and in the Scriptures we read "Except the Lord build the House, the workman worketh in vain." So the magician in all humility seeks the Knowledge and Conversation of his Holy Guardian Angel – that True Self of which his earthly personality is but the mask.

This is the supreme aim of the magician. All else, spells and charms, rituals and circles, swords, wands and fumigations, all are but the means by which he may accomplish that end. Then, being united with that True Self – if only for a brief time – he is instructed by that Inner Ruler in that Higher Magic which will one day bring up his manhood into his Godhood and will achieve that which the True Mysteries have ever declared to be the true end of man – Deification.

# CHAPTER 4

## THE APPARATUS OF MAGIC

IT is only natural, perhaps, that the apparatus of the magical art should have caught the imagination of beholders, and it is in this word "imagination" that the key to the *use* of the various "props" employed by the magician is to be found. In this business of "causing changes in consciousness at will," the right use of the imagination is of the first importance. Let us then consider this faculty of imagination.

It may be defined as the power of the mind to form mental images. From this definition it will be seen that the strictures passed upon its use by the so-called "practical man of the world" are wide of the mark, for anything which is to be carried out into practical effect *must* start as an imaginative picture. What the "practical man" meant, of course, was that any imaginative effort, which did not immediately result in material gain, was a waste of time and effort. But here again, such an idea is far from the truth, for, many imaginations, which have never brought gain directly, have nevertheless opened up channels whereby such advantages might accrue and have also resulted in lasting social and political achievements.

It is evident, therefore, that the "practical man" is not the best authority. What does the psychologist have to say? He deals with the mind in his daily work and may be able to give us a truer picture.

Let us revert for a moment to our consideration of the human personality. We divided it into three levels – the conscious subconscious and superconscious levels, and suggested that the latter two were of greater importance than the ordinary conscious mind. But nevertheless, the conscious mind is that part of the mind with which we are working and evolving upon this planet, and for this reason it must be the directing authority in any attempt at mental and magical work. Allowing it this authority we must also define the limits of its authority. It can and should direct, *but the actual work must be done at the subconscious level.*

The subconscious mind is older, in terms of evolutionary development than the conscious mind, and it retains one trait of its immemorial past in the fact that, as we have said before, it works by *images,* not words. Each of the five physical senses reporting to the brain sends in a series of images visual, tactile, audible, olfactory or gustatory, and these images are linked up in the subconscious mind with their appropriate emotions. If, therefore, one consciously introduces carefully selected images into the subconscious mind one can evoke the corresponding emotion.

Since the emotions are the subjective aspects of the driving energy, which wells up from the deeper levels of the mind, it is evident that by the right use of such conscious evocation the "potential," or pressure of life in the personality, can be greatly enhanced. We see this in a perverted form in the abnormal strength shown by some lunatics during their insane periods, or again, in a higher and more admirable form in the way in which we rise to the occasion of a sudden peril and perform feats which would be impossible to us under ordinary conditions. The phenomena of hypnosis introduce us to the same thing under conditions that allow us to study it at will. In hypnosis we find that, once the barrier or "threshold" has been pierced, and the subconscious levels allowed to emerge above it, any images introduced at this time will have a direct effect upon the dynamism of the personality.

In many systems of mystical and occult thought appropriated from Eastern sources, great stress is laid upon the importance of meditation, and the Eastern Yoga systems are advocated as training methods. Whatever may be the advantages of Yoga, the disadvantage of the application of *Eastern Yoga* to *Western* bodies is found in practice to be considerable, and for that reason, if the Western magician uses the Yoga technique, he employs a modified system which has been adapted to Western use.

In the purely mental methods of meditation there is an insistence upon the control and inhibition of the bodily senses – one is told that it is necessary to be able to shut out unwanted thoughts, to keep the mind unwaveringly fixed upon one thought only, and to refuse to allow any sense impressions to distract one from the chosen object of thought.

In the magical system, however, the images pouring into the mind from the various senses are used as "suggestions" to the conscious mind, which, because of the particularly sensitive condition that has been induced in it by the ritual itself, continues to follow the line upon which it is concentrating. It is a form of psychic *ju-jitsu,* in which the very power of the sense-impressions is used to render the conscious mind immune to their distractions.

Before, however, such images can produce such an effect, two things must be done. The mind must first be "conditioned" to the image. Consciously and persistently the image must be held in the mind and the appropriate emotion associated with it, until, the image being held in the mind, the emotion automatically wells up from the subconscious level. Secondly, either by the actual performance of the ritual, or by some form of auto-hypnosis, the threshold of consciousness must be lowered, so that the subconscious levels emerge into consciousness and become available to the suggestive power of the chosen thought.

So with all magical "props" – the sword, the wand, the pentacle, the cup, the circles, triangles and sigils, the lights, the robes, the incense, the sonorous words of invocation and the "barbarous names" of evocation – all work by a cumulative suggestive process upon the subconscious mind. Such a cumulative suggestion results in what may be termed a mental change of gear, and therefore conforms to our earlier definition of magic as the "Art of causing changes in consciousness at will."

The levels of consciousness reached will depend upon the symbols, etc., used, and also on the amount of conscious association of ideas, which the student has put into it. Magic, far from being an irrational superstition is based, as will be observed, upon profound psychological laws, and possesses its own special technique. With Eastern magical systems we are not here concerned, since this book is written for Western people, and is based upon the theory and practice of the Western Schools.

The "Western Tradition," to give it its technical name, is a composite thing, embracing the magical techniques of all the countries of the Mediterranean Basin on the one hand, and the indigenous system of the Norse and Keltic peoples. The average man, if he takes the trouble to discuss magic, usually has a preconceived idea based upon the fragments of magical practice of the Middle Ages in Europe. Such fragments from the magical "Grimoires" give a very imperfect picture of what the Western Magic is, but they are usually used by our critics as proof of the foolishness and superstition of the practitioners of Magic. However, the same line of argument could be followed by any critic of, say, the Roman Church, and, in fact, the very contemptuous term "Hocus Pocus" which is generally directed against magical practices is the Protestant distortion of the most solemn part of the Christian Eucharist

– *Hoc Est Enim Corpus Meum* – "This is My Body." It was because of certain abuses and superstitions that this word of opprobrium was directed alike against Roman Catholic priest and magical adept.

It is, however, a truer and more equable criterion if we consider the best, and not the worst, in any human institution. Quite apart from any claim which might be made by the Catholic Church to be a supernaturally organised body, or by the magical adepts that they possess a wisdom which has been handed down "from time immemorial," it is evident that their respective organisations are composed of fallible human beings, whose failings and imperfections must inevitably affect the presentation of their beliefs and doctrines.

The Western Tradition affirms of itself that it is the heir to a body of teaching and practice which has been handed down from remote antiquity, and that the central philosophy around which it is organised is the body of Hebrew mystical teaching known as the Qabalah. This word in itself conveys the idea of secrecy, since it signifies the oral transmission of knowledge "from mouth to ear," and indeed, this oral tradition long antedated the public compilation and appearance of such works as the *Sepher Yetzirah,* one of the standard Qabalistic works.

In all the ancient systems of mystical and magical training we find that together with certain philosophical teachings there is to be found a symbol or group of symbols, which has a specialised significance for the followers of that system. Such symbols are known in the East as "Mandalas," and some are exceedingly intricate.

In the Western Tradition, the glyph or composite symbol which is the basis of all its mystical teaching is the diagram known as the Tree of Life and this glyph is described as "The mighty all-embracing Glyph of the Universe and the Soul of Man." It is upon the Tree of Life that the whole of the elaborate detail of ceremonial magic in the West is based. If, for example, the magician is attempting an operation of Jupiter, he will use such properties as are associated with Jupiter on the Tree. He will, for instance, wear a light-blue robe, burn cedar in his censer, have four lighted candles, and use the Hebrew name of the Sphere of Jupiter.

It will be noticed that the magician is using the principle of "association of ideas" but it is necessary to point out that such association of ideas depends in the first place upon a mental link between the various details and the central idea. Now this link may be made voluntarily or involuntarily. In the first case it is made by consciously and deliberately associating the ideas; in the second, the association is immediate and subconscious. Tying a knot in one's handkerchief as a reminder that one has to buy some particular thing, is an example of the first class, whilst the association between, say, sausages and airships is a natural example of the second class. Such involuntary associations often appear to be far more powerful than the deliberately willed ones, for they represent the direct workings of the subconscious mind.

But the willed-association links can be just as powerful if they are correctly built up, and it is this deliberate training of the pictorial imagination which is the basis of the practice of the magician. By this deliberate training it becomes possible for him to link certain pictorial or sensory images with their corresponding emotions, and the consciously directed association causes the appropriate emotional response to appear whenever the sensory images are received. All this, however, is still on the surface of consciousness.

If we wish our association-train to work with the power of magical evocation, then we must use some device to imprint it upon the deeper levels of the subconscious, where it will be able to produce definite results. For this purpose some auto-hypnotic device may be employed, such as, for instance, the use of a rosary or even the meditative repetition of the ritual itself. The rosary, of course, is usually associated with the Roman Catholic Church, but both Mohammedans and Buddhists use the rosary as a device for concentration. Another technical auto-hypnotic device is the use of what are known as the "Flashing Colours."

But before evocation of the subconscious can be safely performed, it is necessary that some work should have been put in on the foundation of character, and this work will be discussed in our next chapter.

# CHAPTER 5

## THE KINGS OF EDOM

CHARACTER training, to the magician, is something very different from that which the ordinary man considers it to be, for the magical character-training involves the willed and purposive re-education of both the conscious and subconscious minds. Ordinary methods of character building usually concentrate almost entirely upon the conscious mind, the subconscious levels being affected only slightly, if at all. It must not be thought, however, that the magician is biassed in the opposite direction. He cultivates conscious and subconscious levels alike, but since he realises that the subconscious is the greater part of the mind, he naturally tends to give it the greater part of his attention.

When, following the occult maxim, the magician turns his mental gaze inwards upon his own personality, he finds, as we said before, that this personality is imperfect and to a large extent inchoate, and he realises that before a true superstructure can be built it will be necessary to pull down much of the present edifice. The question then arises how much can safely be demolished, and what shall be the test as to which part shall be broken down, and which part retained?

This involves the consideration of what constitutes evil, since it is evident that it is the evil aspects of the personality which have to be broken down. But how shall we be able to define evil? Many things that are regarded by some people as "evil" are not so regarded by others! Is there any basic test by which we may judge? The answer is that there is such a test, which is set forth in the Qabalistic systems in the story of Abram and the Kings of Edom. The legend is to be found in Genesis, Chapter XIV, and for the purpose of this book we may briefly summarise it here. Those who prefer to do so may then read the fuller account.

Briefly, Abram was leagued with certain kings in their fight against four other tribal rulers, and on learning that his nephew had been captured by the enemy, Abram fitted out a punitive expedition of his own and defeated the opposing forces, releasing his nephew in the process. Those against whom he fought are termed the "Kings of Edom," and in the Qabalistic books are referred to as "those who reigned before there was a King in Israel."

On his return from the slaughter of the Kings, Abram was met by that mysterious being Melchizedek, King of Salem, Priest of the Most High God, who administered to him the mystic Eucharist of Bread and Wine and blessed him. In the Epistle to the Hebrews, this Melchizedek is described as "without father or mother, having neither beginning of days nor ending of life, he abideth a Priest forever." In all probability the story can be taken at its face value. The nomadic chieftain Abram in alliance with others: defeats the common enemy, and is blessed by the local priest.

The Qabalists, however, regarded the books of the Old Testament in a somewhat different way. The Torah, the Divine "Nemos," as it was written, was the Body of the Law, but just as the body is inert and useless unless it is ensouled, so the written Law was useless without its informing spirit – the Qabalah. So in this story of Abram and the Kings of Edom, each character represents some part of the human personality, and the action of the story shows the interplay of those parts of the mind.

Before considering the esoteric and magical application of the story let us consider the problem of evil in itself, What is "evil"? The magical doctrine is that there are several kinds of evil, some of which, to use a paradox, are not evil! The first type of evil is the innate resistance of form to force. Organised form imposes restrictions upon free-moving force, but this very restriction and opposition enables the force to be controlled and directed. In physical life we observe that the friction between the foot and the ground enables us to move forward – in a frictionless world walking would be impossible and force ineffective – and this principle of restriction works in other fields. By the restriction of boiler and cylinder and piston, steam is harnessed and made to do useful work. So this evil of "inertia" is in reality no true evil, but part of the machinery of this evolving universe.

There is, however, a form of inertia that goes beyond this normal and beneficial one, and this form may truly be called evil. It is the inertia of formlessness and chaos – the "Abortion of Space," the Cosmic Quicksands. Here there is no definite resistance – no springboard from which life can climb to greater heights. But just as the shifting sands of the quicksands though providing no "take-off" yet will cling to, and impede and finally draw down into their depths whatever trusts to them, so is it with the cosmic chaos. Evolving life, finding no resistance, no fulcrum for its lever, may be absorbed and rendered impotent in this "Chaos and Darkness and the Gates of the Land of Night."

A third form of "evil" is that which is termed "unbalanced force." Here a perfectly good and useful force or energy is displaced in space or time and the resulting out-of-balance is definitely evil. Let us consider one or two examples of such unbalanced force.

The coal in the grate is serving a useful and beneficial purpose, giving warmth to the room. Should it fall out upon the carpet, however, it immediately becomes evil. It sets the room alight, damages property, and possibly causes loss of life. The water in the bath is good, but the same water escaping from the bath and cascading down the stairway, is evil. These two instances may serve as illustrations of displacement in space. There is also displacement in time. This may be of two kinds, reversion to the past, or anticipation of the future.

Reversion to the moral and ethical standards of a lower and primitive level of human culture is, to the modern civilised man "evil," since it is a definite regression in evolution. But it is equally evil if, with the limitations and mental outlook of the present day, a person reaches out too far into the future, and attempts to materialise in the conditions of the twenty-first century, the state of civilisation that will possibly be the norm of the peoples of, say, ten thousand years hence. To use an expressive remark the present writer heard the other day, "the lion may lie down with the lamb, ultimately – but he will need his digestive arrangements radically altered!"

This over-anticipation of the future is the fallacy underlying the pacifist attitude. Since the pacifist attitude is only practicable in a well-policed community, it is clearly untenable as a working policy at the present time. Those who may feel that this is a cynical condemnation of what has been taught by the great religious teachers we would refer to the Catholic "Counsels of Perfection." Always the ideal of the future must be pointed to, but although that vision will be the inspiring force tending towards its own realisation, the premature establishment of such conditions is evil.

These types of evil may be termed positive evil, but there is also what may be called positive positive evil. Here we come to a point, which in these modern days is often overlooked – the existence of *organised* evil. It seems as though the materialistic "hang-over" from the nineteenth century has raised some unconscious inhibition in the minds of modern men, so that it is extremely difficult for them to realise that organised evil can and does exist, both on the physical and superphysical levels.

The calculated beastliness revealed during the second
World War should have opened the eyes of some of our
idealists to the possibility of organised evil. We say "should
have," advisedly, since some friends of our – idealists to the
core – told us recently that all the stories of atrocities were
absolutely without foundation, all were merely propaganda,
since "no one could be so evil as to do such things!" It was
suggested that they should attend the courts and listen to a little
of the evidence given there in some of the more sordid cases
which come up for trial in this country. The suggestion was
declined with a display of emotion that suggested that the Old
Adam was not entirely extinct in even their pacifist breasts!

All the old religions have taught of organised spiritual evil,
and the Christian Faith has personified it as Satan. St. Paul
speaks of such organised evil on the superphysical levels when
he says "For we wrestle not against flesh and blood, but against
Principalities, against Powers, against the Rulers of the Darkness
of this present world, against the Spirits of Wickedness in the
Exalted Places" (Eph.: Chapter VI, verse 12).

In the process of the evolution of the Universe energy
of various types has been mis-placed and has been added to
the mis-directed thought of the whole of evolving humanity,
throughout the ages. So the psychic atmosphere of this planet
periodically becomes charged and over-clouded by the "evil"
vibrations until at certain points in time, the evolving life is
checked. It is then that great souls come to earth to recall the
minds of men to the ways of wisdom and the paths of peace,
and to "lift a little of the heavy burden of the sin and suffering
of the world."

The most momentous and significant of these evolutionary
cycles came some two thousand years ago, when the nadir of
the descent of life into form was reached, and the whole of
the manifesting life was in danger of being totally checked

and thwarted. Then came He, the incarnate manifestation of the Logos, the Lord of Light, and through His identification of Himself with the whole human race, He gathered up into Himself all the evil conditions of the planet, and by the Power that was His, He transmuted them into higher conditions and influences – a World Alchemy!

So, too, by His life and death, He established a line of direct contact between the Transcendent God and evolving humanity, along which there might flow into the world-soul the regenerating divine forces, and thus "a new and living way" was made, whereby mankind might enter into the Most Holy Place.

In the parable of the Prodigal Son, we find that not only did the Prodigal set out on his long and painful journey home, but that when he was yet a long way off, his Father saw him, and ran to meet him. So the transcendent Logos hastens to His evolving children as they tread the path that all humanity must tread, and so the Lord of Love, Who is also the Lord of the Balance, gives equilibrium to the unbalanced forces of the universe. So is it also in the heart of each individual, and for this reason the magical student is told in one ritual that he may receive the holy Bread of Life Everlasting and the Chalice of Eternal Salvation "when you shall have slain the Kings of Unbalanced Force in your own nature."

This acquisition of balance is of paramount importance for anyone who desires to operate the Higher Magic whereby his indwelling spirit may manifest itself through the veil of the earthly tabernacle, and it is for this reason, too, that in the Eastern Tradition it is said that "Discrimination is the first virtue of the Path." For the power of the indwelling light, pouring through into the lower personality energises and activates all its levels, good and bad; dissociated complexes explode, as it were, and the whole psychic and mental nature is thrown into ferment. So, therefore, whosoever unworthy and with

unbalanced personality drinks of the Grail of the Holy
Guardian Angel drinks to his own condemnation, as the mighty
forces he has invoked tear through him, inflating his false
egoic sense, intensifying his unbalanced passions and finally
commencing the disintegration of the personality itself. For
such a one, his symbol is "The Blasted Tower," for the house
of his life is destroyed by the Fire of Heaven and he goes forth,
"fleeing where none pursueth," a Son of Perdition, a Wandering
Star, for whom is reserved the Blackness of Darkness for the
Ages of the Ages.

That such a fate awaits *all* who essay the magical art, is,
of course, untrue, and as a matter of observation, the magical
rituals, properly used can be of the greatest assistance in
producing that state of inner equilibrium which is the basis of
the Great Work. The neophyte is cautioned that above all things
he must cultivate true humility – not the humility of Uriah
Heep – but the humility of Him who said "I am amongst you
as One who serves." In the first grade of certain Mysteries, the
neophyte approaches the East in the ritual position of humility,
head bowed and palms outwards turned, and he is instructed
that only by self-less service of the Light can he gain power
to go forward into the Most Holy Place.

# CHAPTER 6

## INVOCATION AND EVOCATION

"I can call spirits from the vasty deep," exclaimed one of Shakespeare's characters, to which his friend replied, "Why, so can I, and so can any man; but will they come when they are called?" This is, of course, the crux of the matter. The average man in the street has a very sceptical approach to the subject and would unhesitatingly answer the question with an emphatic "No!" and regard the attempts of the misguided magician as vanity. Popular superstition has also envisaged the magician as one who conjured, or claimed to conjure the inhabitants of the invisible worlds.

Bearing in mind our definition of Magic, as the art of causing changes in consciousness at will, it becomes evident that we must first consider the whole question of invocation and evocation from the subjective viewpoint. In other words, assuming for a moment that it is possible for the magician to "conjure to visible appearance" beings of another order of existence, we must attempt to show that it is the personality of the magician himself which is the channel through which such manifestation is brought about.

It is a cardinal principle in the Western esoteric schools, that the planes of nature are *discrete*, not continuous, i.e., that each plane of existence has its own laws and its own peculiar method of working, and does not exert a direct influence upon any other plane. Whatever influence is exerted is of indirect or "inductive" nature. The phenomenon of electrical induction furnishes a very close parallel to this statement. If a coil of wire carrying an alternating current or a varying current is brought close to, but not touching, a similar coil of wire, which is connected to a galvanometer and is not carrying any current, it will be found that as the current-carrying coil is brought near the other, the meter will record that a current of electricity has been generated in the latter.

Furthermore it will be found, if a galvanometer be placed in the current-carrying coil, that if the second coil has its resistance to electricity altered, the free flow of the current in the first or "primary" coil will be either checked or increased, showing that both coils act upon each other. So it is with the planes of existence. The higher is negative or *receptive* to that which is higher than itself, and positive or *dynamic* towards that which is lower. But equally, the lower reacts upon the higher, and this is the justification for the Biblical statement that the Kingdom of Heaven "suffereth violence, and is taken by storm."

Now it has been found by experience that the levels can come into direct contact with each other through the lens of an organised consciousness of some kind or other. The best point of contact that can be found is a trained and balanced human consciousness. The human mind contains within itself the vibration-rates of all the planes, and by tapping it at certain points a link-up may be made with the existence of that level. It is a process of "tuning-in" such as is used in wireless, and once again the electrical analogy is very close. When we tune in to our favourite radio programme, whatever it may be, we do not hear the actual voice of the singer, or the actual sound of the instrument. What we hear is a *reproduction,* a projected reproduction of the actual voice or sound.

So it is in evocation and invocation. We make contact through our own energised consciousness with the consciousness of the beings we seek to evoke and the "visible appearance" we conjure up is a *projection* from our own mind. (So, for the matter of that, is the visible image we form when we use our physical eyes! The light vibrations strike the retina, set up nervous impulses in the optic centre and we project a mental image answering to those impulses.)

In both cases, however, this reaction is caused by an *objective* reality of some kind, whether physical or superphysical, and here we come to what may be termed the "objective" viewpoint. The magical tradition declares that all these existences exist *per se* and have their own place in Nature. But – and this is important – the appearances which are seen are conditioned by the subjective mental machinery of the magician himself. Through this machinery also, the actual power and energy of the invisibles is brought through into the waking consciousness. (Not that the *identical* power of the invisibles is brought through, but rather the effect of the contact of the consciousness of the magician with that of the being invoked or evoked arouses into activity the corresponding force within himself, and it is this corresponding power which is projected and which produces the results desired.)

It is important to note the difference between "invocation" and "evocation." In invocation we act in such a way as to attract the attention of some Being of a superior nature to our own, or some cosmic force of a higher order. In evocation we impose our will upon beings of a lesser order of existence and compel them to execute our wishes. In both cases the actual contact takes place through our own mental channel, but a magical technique has been devised whereby the essential difference between the two sets of influences – the higher and the lower – is kept before the magician. The reason for this is that should there be any confusion in the mind of the magician, the results may be disastrous.

For a moment let us consider this from the psychological point of view. If the forces, or Beings, summoned by invocation represent the super-conscious part of the mind, then the Beings who answer the evocatory commands of the adept represent – or rather work through – the subconscious levels. But whilst the supraconscious contacts tend towards a greater and more effective integration of the mind, the subconscious ones tend, if not controlled, to bring about its partial or total disintegration, as C. G. Jung has pointed out. So the Magical Tradition has evolved the technical devices known as the "Circle of Safety" and the "Triangle of Art," the whole being termed the "Place of Working."

By certain rituals, the place where the magical work is to be performed is purified etherically on the objective plane, and psychologically on the subjective one, and the Circle of Safety is drawn upon the floor as a kind of fortress from within which the magician may work. Then the Triangle of Art is drawn outside the Circle, for in the case of evocation it is necessary that the objective manifestation of the beings evoked should be kept within its limits and under rigid control, and in the mind of the operator there should be a clear-cut psychological distinction between himself as the positive or dominant and the lesser forces or beings which are negative to him.

The purification of the Place of Working is done in the Western Magic by what is known as the Banishing Ritual of the Lesser Pentagram, or in other cases by the Ritual of the Hexagram. The Lesser Pentagram ritual is more often used, and the present writer, who has performed it on many occasions, can vouch for its efficiency. It is a combination of geometric signs made by the operator, Names of Power which are intoned by him, certain mental images which are visualised very strongly, and the definite invocation of certain Arch-Angelic Powers.

Again, looking at this from the psychological angle, we are asserting by word and sign the sovereignty of the Higher Self, whilst by the invocations, we draw down upon ourselves certain of its powers – powers which are released by the action of existences of another order upon it.

In the greater number of cases the invocation or evocation "to visible appearance" is to psychic vision only, and nothing is seen upon the physical plane. Where material visibility ensues, we have another process at work, and this is the process of "materialisation." For such materialisation to take place, it is necessary that there should be present some source of the peculiar substance termed by the spiritualists, "ectoplasm." One such source, and that the most effective, is the bodily organism of one of the people known to the spiritualists as "materialisation mediums." They are people who possess a certain little-understood power that enables them to give out this ectoplasm in large quantities. Ectoplasm is so named because it is a peculiar plasma or living substance, which is exuded from, and manifests outside of the physical organism of the medium.

It appears to be capable of being moulded by thought and desire into forms – in fact, one of its characteristics is an innate tendency towards organisation. The data so far obtained by the spiritualists and by open-minded observers such as Sir William Crookes, Baron Shrenck-Notzing and Dr.W.J.Crawford suggest that this ectoplasm is the basic substance of living protoplasm, and as such is the matrix of the physical organism.

We find, however, that there are other sources of ectoplasm, though it is of a different type and is given off in small quantities only. Before passing on to these sources, we may briefly mention one method of obtaining sufficient ectoplasm for a materialisation to take place. This method is the use of fresh animal blood. It is a method known throughout history and is referred to by Homer. There is an obscure Gnostic legend which says that the golden bells worn upon the dress of the Jewish High-Priest were designed to warn the beings evoked by the blood sacrifices of the Temple to assume human shape instead of their own grotesque forms. Anyone who takes the trouble to study the details of the temple sacrifices will appreciate the force of this legend, and will also become convinced that there was sufficient blood for any materialisation.

One can vouch for the efficacy of freshly spilt blood as a basis of such materialisation. Quite recently a case of "haunting" investigated by the present writer proved to have, as its basis of manifestation just such blood emanations. Once the material basis was removed, the manifestations ceased to be objective and the subjective psychic atmosphere was easily cleared by a banishing ritual. We may note in passing that many cases of hauntings are due to the efforts of a so-called "dead" person to make contact with the world he or she has left behind, and the spiritualists have developed a very effective technique which allows the discarnate person an opportunity to make a conscious contact with those on the earth who are able, by their knowledge of psychic matters, to help in the necessary adjustment of the new conditions of life.

Returning to our consideration of the sources of ectoplasm other than materialisation mediums or the emanations of blood, the one commonly used in magical rites is a peculiar incense known as Dittany of Crete. Fresh flowers also give off an appreciable amount of this substance in a rarified form, as do also the naked flames of candles. In normal magical work, the blood rites are never used, and the use of a medium is also eschewed because of the depletion of vitality that may result. The use of the incense is free from the disadvantages of these two methods, but the forms which are "evoked to visible appearance," although clearly perceptible to normal vision do not possess the solidity of those produced by the former methods.

Although the evocation to visible appearance is one of the more spectacular feats of the magical art, it is not often resorted to, as for the majority of purposes it is sufficient if the "visible appearance" is to psychic vision only. It is sufficient if the operator is enabled to perceive objectively the beings evoked – conscious comprehension and direct perception of them giving the magician power over them. Once again we find a parallel in the psychological field, the dissociated or repressed "complexes" in the mind are controlled by the conscious realisation of them. Moreover, when spirits of a "good" nature are evoked, we can again resort to the psychological clue, for it is a fact that the clear realisation of a mental faculty results in the rapid development of that faculty in the individual concerned. And such a subjective realisation means also that by virtue of a law of sympathetic induction, we come into contact with objective beings and forces of a similar type existing in the inner worlds. It is this that gives validity to such statements in the mediaeval "grimoires" or magical books as "The Spirits of Mercury give understanding of science."

Having completed the evocation, it becomes necessary to dismiss the beings evoked. We may employ an electrical analogy here and say that it is necessary to discharge our charged circle, to "earth" it, and so return our evoked force to its normal place in the natural economy. This dismissal is performed by "The license to depart." Here is a typical charge of dismissal. The magician makes upon himself the Kabbalistic Cross, and addresses the beings he has invoked thus:

Because ye have duly appeared unto us, and performed that with which ye were charged; depart now in peace to your own habitations. Peace be between us; be ye very ready to again obey the summons, and may the blessing of Adonai be upon you as ye may be able to receive it.

The magician then proceeds, by the technical device of the "Closing of the Gate," to withdraw his attention both conscious and subconscious from the inner plane levels and to re-focus upon the physical plane. This is most important, as it prevents the disintegration of the mind, which results from the habitual uncontrolled evocation of the subconscious. Where the magician has been invoking higher intelligences, the license to depart is unnecessary, but the Closing of the Gate is important just the same. It is stated by certain authorities that in the Eucharist the words *Ita missa est* at the end of the service are, in effect, not a license to depart, but a statement to the angelic Beings who have taken part in the service that their work is now concluded. It is not a peremptory dismissal.

# CHAPTER 7

## MAGNETIC MAGIC

WHEN Dr. Mesmer first attracted international attention in the Eighteenth century by his remarkable cures and his peculiar doctrines, the Western world was just beginning the serious study of the more recondite forces of Nature such as electricity, magnetism and gravity.

Mesmer, in the thesis which gained for him his doctorate, outlined a theory of the universe which was, and still is, that of the Western Esoteric Tradition, though in its public form it had of necessity only a shadow of its real content. Briefly, Mesmer saw the whole universe as a living unity; wherein each part was affected by and in its turn affected every other part. The universe was a living organism of balancing forces. Health, therefore, lay in each part so adjusting itself to every other part that it received to the fullest of its capacity the directing, controlling and sustaining life of the whole.

He taught that this formative life could be transmitted from one being to another, and he claimed also that its force was operative behind and apart from the physical plane energies, which were being studied by the scientific world. Particularly, asserted Mesmer, did this universal force manifest behind and through the phenomena of magnetism. He used bar magnets which he claimed possessed curative power because of this universal force, but later both he and his followers taught that it was also thrown off freely from the human organism. It was therefore named "animal magnetism," and the school of the animal magnetists, chief amongst them being such men as de Puysegar and Baron du Potet developed their theories and practice along this line.

When Dr. James Braid put forward his own theory of "Hypnotism,"* and later when the followers of Charcot and the members of the so-called "Nancy School" put forward the theory of "Suggestion," Mesmer's "fluid" theory was discarded and the very idea of animal magnetism was deemed ridiculous. But though it was respectable to deny the existence of the magnetic fluid, there were many who quietly worked along the lines indicated by Mesmer and. du Potet. One of the notable names in this connection is that of Baron Reichenbach who conducted an exhaustive enquiry into what he called "Odic Force," or, more briefly, "Od." His researches clearly established the existence of a force that underlies all natural forces.

Thus, the sensitive people who acted as his observers could see, in total darkness, a "flame" as they called it, emanating from the end of a wire the other end of which was exposed to strong sunlight or moonlight. Experiment showed that if the exposed end of the wire was shielded the observers noted the disappearance of the odic flame, though they were entirely unaware of any change in the conditions of the experiment. It was observed that similar odic flames were associated with the poles of both electromagnets and permanent magnets. The human body was seen to be radiating this same force. A touch of humour is to be found in the observation that the human lips also radiated odic energy, and a possible reason was thus suggested for the efficacy of lovers' kisses!

Today, with the researches of Dr. Kilner and the use of very

---

* A modern investigation into this subject is to be found in *Proceedings of the Society for Psychical Research,* Vol. XXXII. July, 1921, in a paper "Problems of Hypnotism" by Dr. Sidney Airutz. Lecturer on Psychology at the University of Upsala.

sensitive electrical measuring instruments, the existence of this odic force is being more and more accepted. We may use the name "magnetism," providing that we make it clear that this "magnetism" has nothing to do with the magnetism studied by physicists and electricians, even though it may be associated with it. This animal magnetism, therefore, is an actual force or energy thrown off automatically by the healthy animal and the healthy human alike, but it is capable of being consciously developed and intensified, and it is this intensified and directed power which is the basis of the branch of magic with which we are now dealing.

It will help the reader to understand the magnetic phenomena if he thinks of this force as the "magnetic fluid," remembering that the French term is more comprehensive than the English word "fluid." Perhaps the phenomena of radium may afford some analogy. It is known that from a small speck of radium there are innumerable small particles radiating in a constant stream, and this stream is measurable as a definite force, though it is composed of these extremely small particles.

So the magnetic force is also of the nature of an emanation of extremely refined substance which is directed and controlled by the will and thought of the magnetist. It can be stored – can be attached to or absorbed by certain material objects, whilst other objects will act as insulators to it. Herein it seems to have some indirect relationship to electricity, for most of the *electrical* insulators are also *magnetic* insulators, though there are some puzzling exceptions. All metals are good magnetic conductors; oil and water absorb it readily, though oil retains it for a longer period. Wool and paper, wood, brick and stone absorb it slightly, but silk will neither conduct nor absorb it.

It has been established by careful experiment that the magnetic force tends to reproduce in the object to which it is directed its own particular "vibration or note," and the object will then come into close psychic sympathy or "rapport" with the person who projected the magnetism. Thus, animal

magnetism is the basic power in many forms of psychic and
spiritual healing, being as it were, a healing power in itself and
also acting as a carrier for more subtle forces which through
its agency are enabled to affect the physical body.

It will be remembered that one of the miracles* attributed
to Jesus was the healing of the woman with an issue of blood.
The Gospel story gives a clear picture of the occurrence, the
Teacher standing in the centre of a crowd of people who press
in upon Him, pushing past His disciples who are trying to keep
an open space around Him, and everyone trying to touch even
the hem of His robe. The East does not change rapidly, and
the present writer has often witnessed similar scenes in India.
The Master asks, "Who touched Me?" The amazement of the
disciples is pardonable. Who touched Him? They might well
exclaim. "Who didn't touch Him?" But the record goes on to
say that He perceived that virtue had gone forth from Him.

We have, perhaps, been misled by this word "virtue."
thinking of it only as an ethical thing – "A virtuous woman
is above rubies." But the true meaning of this word is that of
power, so that we also say such-and-such a thing has virtue in
it. (In the Middle Ages, and today in the East, the virgin and the
child without sin are held to possess a power, which is the result
of their purity.) When the word which is translated "virtue" in
the Authorised Version of the Bible is studied, we find that it is
the root-word from which are derived such words as "dynamo,"
"dynamic" and "dynamite," all words implying powerful active
energy. So the Master's query is clear. The woman who had
touched Him had, through the conditions established within
her by her faith become a conductor, or rather an absorbent
of the healing virtue or vital dynamic energy that was radiating
from Him. Many a magnetic healer at the present day can
echo that statement in the Gospel, for they, too, perceive that
virtue has gone forth from them. Father John of Cronstadt

---

* Cf the definition of "miracles" given by St. Augustine, "Miracles are not
contrary to Nature, but only contrary to what we know about Nature."

and Father Mathew, an Irish priest, both died prematurely as a result of their excessive work. It is interesting to note that Father Mathew received an annuity of £300 per year from Queen Victoria, in recognition of his services.[*]

In magical work, this magnetic power is made use of in many ways. It is used for healing by charging or impregnating a handkerchief or other article with healing power, this "charged" object being worn or used by the sick person. Sometimes, water is similarly charged, or oil; sometimes crosses, pendants or other personally worn articles are charged or "magnetised" to use the technical term. In the New Testament we read of people taking cloths which had been in the vicinity of St. Paul to sick people, and the practice of charging or "blessing" objects has never ceased in the Catholic Churches of both the Western and Eastern Obediences

It is important to remember that the magnetic fluid is neutral in itself, and will take upon itself the impress of the mind and will that sent it forth. Like all the bodily forces, it is manipulated by the subconscious mind, and since the subconscious responds most readily to pictorial suggestion from the conscious mind, the magician has to have a stock of clear-cut mental images to which the subconscious mind has already been emotionally linked or "conditioned." Such a stock of images is found, for instance, in the Qabalistic Tree of Life, which is the training glyph of the Western magician; in the East, other glyphs or composite symbols are used.

The process of magnetising an object falls into two divisions, de-magnetising or "exorcising," and magnetising or "blessing." A third process is what is known as "consecration," but this involves other factors, as will be seen. The de-magnetisation is performed by holding in the

---

[*] Cf Dr. Percy Dearmer's *Body and Soul* for a learned study of this form of healing.

mind the intention to purify the object, and the magnetism of the operator is directed upon it by one or other of the traditional signs of power. In the Catholic Church exorcism is performed through the sign of the cross. The Qabalist also uses the Cross, but it is important to notice that this is the *equal-armed Cross of the Elements,* not the Latin form. A traditional form of words is used, and the general formulae of the Catholic priest and the Qabalist are very similar – probably due to the influence of mediaeval times, when it often happened that the priest carried on a certain amount of magical work in addition to his ordinary clerical duties. Lapsed priests who followed the magical tradition would almost of necessity adapt their familiar formulae to the new work, and the educated magician altered such formulae to suit his own purposes. In any case, the Roman Church, with its amazing versatility absorbed much of the magical traditions of the cults it superseded, and, as Evelyn Underhill points out in her valuable work *Mysticism,* the truly Hermetic employment of lights and salt and water and oil in the baptismal service is far removed from the simple lustrations of St. John the Baptist.

Having demagnetised or exorcised the object, we have it now in a neutral condition, ready to absorb any magnetic force that may be impressed upon it. Now the process of magnetisation begins. Again the operator must have in his mind a certain "intention," and this intention must be expressed in words and manual acts which are linked in his mind with the desired action of the charged object. Together with this, the magician employs a certain technical mental device known as "commemoration." This consists of a recital of similar work performed by others in the past, and serves to link the operator with the archetypal images in the collective consciousness of the race, thus reinforcing the individual powers of the magician. Whether the events commemorated actually occurred or not makes no difference to their efficacy if they are part of the folklore or mythology of the race.

It is important to note that the ideas and images that are held in the operator's mind must be positive, *never* negative. Thus, if we were charging or blessing an object for the purpose of reinforcing the courage of the person using it, we should fill our minds with the pictures of courage, not fear. We should not say, "Let the wearer of this cease from being afraid," but rather, "Let the wearer of this be strong and of good courage," and we should use a form of words which would reiterate this idea. In fact we should proceed as if we were giving suggestion to the person concerned directly.

We spoke of consecration as a technical method embodying other factors. In the normal magnetisation of objects the powers and forces of the personality of the operator are utilised, but in consecration, after the object has been de-magnetised it is re-magnetised with a special intention that it may be the vehicle or channel of a higher force or being apart altogether from the operator. A typical consecration ritual is the Mass of the Catholic Church. Here we have all the elements we have mentioned, the purification of the bread and wine, their solemn blessing and setting-apart, and then in the Prayer of Consecration, the commemoration of the first Eucharist of the Christian Church, and the invocation of the Presence of Christ in and through the offered elements.

In treating of this talismanic magic, and of the much greater "Magic of the Mass," it may be thought that we have departed from our original definition of magic as the art of causing changes of consciousness at will. This is not the case. The effect of the talisman is to effect a change of consciousness – usually in a gradual fashion – in the person using it, and the same applies to the power of the Blessed Sacrament. That the change of consciousness may not be observed by the user matters not. Man's consciousness, as we have seen, is greater than his surface-waking mind.

It is possible that the linking-up of the Eucharist with the subject of magic may cause some disquiet. This should not be the case if the objectors hold sincerely the central doctrine of Christianity. For what was the Incarnation but an act of supreme magic whereby the Word was made flesh and dwelt among us, His transcendent Power flooding the planet on which we live, and, like the leaven in the lump, working throughout the ages to effect a change of consciousness in the whole of humanity!

Talismanic magic was very popular during the Middle Ages, and even the consecrated Host was used for magical purposes. In the first reformed Prayer Book of Edward VI, in 1549, there is a rubric which runs as follows:- "And although … the people these many years past received at the priest's hands the Sacrament of the Body of Christ in their own hands. … yet as they many times conveyed the same secretly away, kept it with them, and diversely abused it to superstition and wickedness…it is thought convenient the people commonly receive the Sacrament of Christ's body in their mouths at the priest's hands."

# CHAPTER 8

## THE MAGICAL IMAGES

THE technical methods of the magical tradition are based, as we have already seen, upon a deep knowledge of the human mind, and in the use of what are called the "magical images" this is clearly seen.

Two very different men have introduced the concept of the magical image to the Western world, St. Ignatius Loyola and C. G. Jung. The first of these in order of time is, of course, St. Ignatius, whose *Spiritual Exercises* are the foundation of the system of mind training and discipline which has produced one of the most effective of the Catholic Orders – the Society of Jesus. Whatever may be one's private opinion of the Jesuits, one thing is certain, they form one of the most effective communities in the Church.

It is sometimes objected to the Jesuit system of training that it is "anthropocentric" in contradistinction to the Sulpician method, which is "theocentric." It is really a matter of temperament – one type turns inward and seeks through knowledge of the self to know the One, the other type seeks through knowledge of the One to understand the self. If one is permitted to use a physical simile, one type is centrifugal and the other centripetal. Just as these two opposing forces produce as their resultant the balanced system of a sun and its planets, so the magical tradition makes use of both the Ignatian and Sulpician methods – in point of fact it was using them long before they were introduced into the Catholic Church.

In modern days, the psychologist Carl G. Jung has shown how important to everyone are what are termed the "archaic images" of the collective unconscious. It will be remembered that in our study of the mind, we spoke of the stratum of the mind that is common to all humanity - a Race Consciousness from which our individual personal consciousnesses rise like mountains from their surrounding ranges. Jung points out that if the normal consciousness "regresses" or turns inward upon itself, it turns the psychic energy loose upon the vast storehouse of the subconscious levels. Now in the magical tradition these subconscious levels are known as "The Treasure-House of Images," and it is upon these images that the inward turned energy proceeds to work.

As these images become active, they tend to rise past the censor at the threshold of the mind and emerge in the conscious levels as dreams and visions and intuitions, moreover they "project" special meanings upon objects and images that have affinity with them. Now it is obvious that the involuntary and pathological regression of neurosis is detrimental to the mental unity that constitutes normal health, though even the regression of the neurotic is an attempt by the deeper levels of the mind to re-establish balanced conditions. But the regression of the magical technique is a voluntary, willed activity whereby the normal mental polarity is deliberately reversed and the stream of psychic energy redirected in accordance with a certain well-defined plan. We may describe this as a system of evocation. But not only is the psychic energy directed into the subconscious levels, it emerges therefrom carrying upon its stream the potent images of the Collective Unconscious, or rather, the "lines of force" of those images.

Perhaps an illustration will make this clear. If a solution of some salt is allowed to crystallise we observe that the substance forms crystals of a certain type, and it is evident that in the solution itself there must already exist the pre-disposing "lines of force" along which the peculiar crystals of the substance form. We may say, therefore, that although six-sided or eight-sided crystals did not *exist* in the solution, there nevertheless was a system of stresses *subsisting* therein, whose manifestation is seen in the solid crystals formed later. So the archaic images of the collective unconscious *subsist* in the deeper levels of the mind, as *systems of stresses,* not *objective* images.

But if the "dead" images of the immemorial past are thus resurrected, with what body do they come? The answer is that that which is "sown" in the conscious mind is not that image which shall arise, but is the link whereby the archaic lines of force are clothed upon and appear in a new "body." But this new body is charged with the power of the regions wherein it had its origin, and the psychic energy that has evoked it is reinforced by this primordial force emanating from spaceless and timeless regions. So mortality puts on immortality and the image, arising in consciousness brings a new power to bear upon the personal self. This resurrection of the Deeper Self results in the regeneration and reconstitution of the personal self. It is the *coagula* portion of the alchemists' formula, and this power is, in Christian terminology the power of the Holy Ghost.

In the psychological technique of Jung and his disciples there are several methods whereby this resurgence may be effected. The magical tradition has also evolved a detailed system of training whereby this evocation of the Images may take place. "Deep calls to Deep," and this is the key to the magical method. It is one of *induction.*

In those magical ceremonials wherein this evocation of the primordial forces is aimed at, carefully selected images are employed. These are chosen from the mass of symbolic images which are to be found in the Qabalistic books, and are used by the magician to build up the mental atmosphere which will evoke from the deeper levels of the mind those archaic images and powers which are desired. Now the archaic images of the collective unconscious tend to group around certain definite centres. As Jung teaches, the motives of the archetypes (archaic images) are the same in all cultures. We find them repeated in all mythologies and fairy-tales, in all religious traditions and mysteries. Prometheus the stealer of fire, Hercules the slayer of dragons, the numerous myths of creation, the fall from Paradise, the sacrificial mysteries, the virgin birth, the betrayal of the hero, the dismembering of Osiris and many other myths and tales portray psychic processes in symbolic-imaginary forms.

Likewise the forms of the snake, the fish, the sphinx, the helpful animals, the World-Tree, the Great Mother, the Enchanted Prince, the mage, the *puer eternus,* stand for certain figures and contents of the collective unconscious. Myths and fairy-tales are the daydreams of the race, and each race has its own particular forms of the common myths. Being aware of this racial selectivity, the magician therefore endeavours to use such images as may be in affinity with the collective mind of the race with which he is dealing. As we have said before, the Western Tradition is a composite one and the Western magician uses one or other of the subordinate systems that it contains.

For example, in this country he works with the Keltic contact and the images of the Grail legend if he desires to avail himself of the power of the Rosicrucian Order. There are very many images which may be used without stepping outside our racial boundaries, and though it is of the greatest advantage to us to be able to avail ourselves of the Eastern systems of philosophy, when it comes to a question of practical magical work, it is best to restrict one's efforts to Western methods. This is not to deprecate Eastern methods which are sound and efficacious for Easterns and for those few who, though born in the West are spiritually of the East.

In conjunction with the glyph which is used by the Qabalists, there are ten magical images which represent the working of the universal energy in all its aspects, and these are used to "tune in" to that energy on the particular level required. This energy, however, is not a blind mechanical force, but a living, pulsating, energy-consciousness, so that if a thought-form or magical image is built up in the conscious mind and linked up with its corresponding archetype in the deeper consciousness, the image that emerges from the depths and floods the waking consciousness with power is a living thing.

If, now, many people over a prolonged period of time build such a mental image, then the individual images appear to coalesce, and we have one image, charged with the Divine Life in one of its aspects. This is what the ancients termed a "god." It is important to note that the objectivisation of such a "god" is through the minds of the worshippers, and what is really happening is that the form or image consciously visualised acts as a line of contact with the collectively-built form, and this in its turn is linked with the cosmic energy it symbolises. The result is that cosmic energy flowing through the mind of the worshipper stimulates the appropriate archetype that rises into consciousness and acts as a transmitter of that energy to all levels of the personality of the worshipper.

That which is done by faith and devotion alone, the magician does with the added knowledge of the mechanism whereby this energy is brought through for the strengthening and refreshing of his soul, and for that willed change in consciousness which we have agreed upon as our definition of magic.

It is important to note that there are two ways of working with the magical images. One of these methods is not to be recommended, as it tends to reduce the power that may be obtained from them. These vast collective thought-forms are "charged" with the emotional energy of their makers, and this stored energy is available for any individual member of the group. We may liken the magical image to the charged batteries of a private house lighting-plant. If the batteries are constantly being drawn upon there comes a point when they fail to deliver power - they are, as we say, discharged. So it is with the magical images. If they are used inexpertly they tend to lose their charge of energy. But no skilled electrician would allow his batteries to become totally discharged, but would start up the dynamo and allow the drain of energy to come upon what is, for practical purposes, an inexhaustible source of power. Neither would the skilled magician use the images as sources of power *in themselves.* He uses them as temporary sources of energy, but always links up *through* them with the infinite power behind all manifestation. This marks the difference between the amateur and the skilled magician, and is one of the reasons why the detailed descriptions of the magical images used in the occult Lodges are kept secret.

Some of the magical images are of great antiquity and are highly charged with psychic energy. They have been built up and used by generations of initiates. Outside the occult Lodges, the great images built by generations of worshippers of the major religions possess great potency and because of their evocative power over the archaic images in the subconscious minds of the people, they are of the greatest possible value to organised religious systems, and those sects which attempt to dispense altogether with ceremonial and imagery are giving up a very valuable weapon in the spiritual armoury.

This brings us to the consideration of the practice of the Catholic Church known as the Invocation of the Saints. Before going any further, it may be pointed out that in the Roman Church three grades of "worship" are recognised. First we have *dulia,* the reverence paid to Saints because of their spiritual greatness; *hyperdulia,* the reverence paid to the Virgin Mary, and *Latria,* the worship paid to Almighty God alone. This by way of disposing of the silly Protestant idea that Catholics give to the Saints and the Lady Mary the worship due to God alone. If we consult the official documents of the Church, we find that there is a point that is of interest to us in our study of the magical images. The Council of Trent, which removed many of the mediaeval abuses of the Roman Church defines the Invocation of the Saints in the following manner:

To worship the Saints means to worship God, for their blessedness and sanctity are really His. And to pray with the Saints means to adore God together with the hierarchies of Angels, with the spirits of the just men made perfect, and with the Church invisible of those who are first-born unto the heaven world. *(Concidium Tridentinum, Sessio XXV. De Invocatione Sanctorum.)*

The point of interest in this passage of the proceedings of the Council is the statement that to worship the saints is to worship God, i.e., it is the power of God shining through the saints which is, shall we say, canalised or concentrated by the personality of the saint. This is, of course, the doctrine of the magical image. But the personality, which is used as the channel, is a *true* personality, a human being who with us worships the same God. So it is that the Saint of the Catholic Church, still remaining a distinct being, nevertheless acts as a psychic lens, focusing and concentrating that ray of the eternal light of which he or she is an especial channel. All who by innate temperament are on this particular ray will be able to draw upon this saint for that power.

This applies not only to the saints of the Church, but to the heroes of folklore. In our own native tradition pagan and Christian heroes and saints are intertwined in the Grail and Arthurian legends. It was the custom at one time, to reduce all these hero figures to myth-personifications and to deny their existence as real men and women. At a later date it was held that they really had existed and that popular thought had clothed them with the garments of myth.

The initiated magician holds that both views are partly right, right that is, in what they affirm, wrong in what they deny, and he believes that the full truth is to be found in a combination of both ideas. When the magical images are being employed in lodges of ceremonial magic, the impersonal cosmic images are used, but by the technical device known as Commemoration, the archetypal images are linked up with the personalities who in their earth-life in the past have exemplified the particular power symbolised and canalised by the magical image concerned.

In order that this power may be brought still further into physical plane conditions, each member of the magical team performs the operation known as "assuming the God-form." He or she "plays the part" of the personality, or Being commemorated as forming the channel of the power of their particular office in the lodge, at the same time attempting to link up through that personality with the cosmic power. Now the method of assuming the God-form is a certain technical method of autohypnosis. When by this operation a lesser change of consciousness has been effected, it is as though a self-starting mechanism has been switched on. The personality of the magician is overshadowed and flooded by the power of his deeper Self, and this is illuminated and charged through the entity who has been commemorated, and through the channel of the linked personalities the cosmic energy rushes down into the psychic and magnetic conditions of the magician. The effect of this downrush of power is to cause the buried archaic images to rise into his temporarily exalted consciousness, and these images allow the invoked power to effect definite and far-reaching changes in the character of the initiate.

Around the ten basic magical images of the Tree of Life there are grouped the gods and goddesses of the pagan pantheons as well as the saints and heroes of myth and legend, and the choice of a particular image depends upon the effect desired. In passing it may be said that each group of Images has a certain affinity with one or other of the great psycho-physiological centres of the human body, and with the particular mental "control-centre" governing each one. The vibrational keynote of each centre determines the traditional words of power connected with the images linked with it. The whole subject of "words of power" is one of great complexity and can only be touched upon briefly here.

A variation of the assumption of the God-form is that curious "illusion technique" referred to in the magical books as "making oneself invisible" and "transformation." Such "glamour" has to be experienced to be realised. A typical instance is given in Col. H. S. Olcott's book *Old Diary Leaves.* Here the protagonists were Madame H. P. Blavatsky and a certain Qabalist.

If this study of the magical images seems a little disjointed, it must be remembered that although one may discuss general principles, it is difficult to be precise without saying too much.

---

* Old Diary Leaves, Vol.1

# CHAPTER 9

## INITIATORY MAGIC

IN the religious rites of all nations from time immemorial, we find certain ceremonies of admission into the tribal membership or the religious life of the nation, and these initiations have certain common elements, whether it be the induction of a boy into the tribe by Australian aborigines or the reception of a postulant into the Catholic Church. Sir James Frazer, in his *Golden Bough*, has brought together many examples of initiatory rites from all over the world, and these, together with such present-day forms of initiation as that of the Masonic Craft and the baptismal rites of the Church all show an underlying similarity.

The word "initiation" is derived from a root signifying "a first step or beginning," and this, of course, is just what initiation is. It is the first step in a new life, whether that life be the tribal life of the clan, the religious life of the monk, the ethical and benevolent life of the modern mason, or the generally benevolent and brotherly activities of the Royal and Antediluvian Order of Buffaloes. All these have their initiatory rites, through which the neophyte is introduced to and linked up with a new life. We may add to these examples two others – the initiatory ceremonies of knighthood and the coronation of the British monarch.

It is obvious that all initiations will not have the same power – that some will affect the candidate at entirely different levels to others – but, and this is a point to be stressed, even the most innocuous and naive of initiatory ceremonies may, if it is built upon true foundations and is worked by men of knowledge, be the means whereby radical and far-reaching changes of consciousness in the postulant may be brought about.

It is a remarkable fact that practically all organised societies sooner or later develop some form of initiatory ceremony, and although this may be considered as due to the natural desire to make a clean break between the old life and the new, it has yet to be explained why the basis of all such initiations seems to be the same. Associated also with these rites we find the "laying on of hands" or some similar act, and it would appear from anthropological research that where such rites commenced without the laying on of hands, the process was nevertheless introduced at an early date.

It will be seen therefore, that there are two essential components of a true initiatory rite. First the severance from the old life dramatised in certain symbolic forms, and secondly the transmission of power to the neophyte. The former is built upon the idea of a departure from blind wanderings in the chaotic and darkened conditions of ignorance into the realms of light and order – the "Coming Forth by Day" of the Egyptian *Book of the Dead,* the "Entrance into the Clear Light" of the Tibetan *Bardo Thodol,* the Royal Transmutation of the Alchemists, the New Birth of the Christian mystics. But each in its degree. For obviously the Masonic initiation has rarely such thaumaturgic effect. Neither have many of the formal initiations of East or West.

Yet some effect is produced, and some power conferred, but it is "under the veil of earthly things." For these formal initiations, valid and valuable though they may be, are the earthly shadows of the true initiations that are conferred in the timeless and spaceless eternities. In the words of the Qabalah, they are "reflections into Malkuth," i.e., the representation in earth terms of supersensible realities. Thus, we are not made adepts by the ceremonial initiations in lodge (though certain powers, as we shall see, do accrue to us as a result of the ceremony), but we become initiated when we have ourselves voluntarily changed our habitual consciousness and begun to look at all things from a different point of view. The word which is translated in the Authorised Version of the Bible as "conversion," is a word which can best be described as meaning "the turning the mind around and regarding of things from another point of view." This, of course, is just what initiation – and conversion – really is.

Here we come to one of the points at issue between the Catholic and Non-conformist. The Church teaches that infant baptism is efficacious and sufficient, the Non-conformists look for a conscious change of heart, taking place in youth or adult life, which brings the person concerned into the true fold. From the occult point of view, both sides are again right in what they affirm and wrong in what they deny.

Baptismal regeneration and conversion are both valid and efficacious and should be complementary to each other. The magical tradition gives a clear explanation of this, and it is reinforced by the findings of the psychoanalysts. In order to understand the magical tradition it will be necessary to study what is known in psychology as "the group mind."

When a number of people associate themselves together in pursuit of a common object, their minds link up together and form - for the purpose they have in mind – a composite or group mind. The more emotional the object of their combined thought, the stronger and more clearly built becomes the group mind. The permanence of the group-mind depends upon many factors; for instance, some group-minds formed by the impassioned oratory of some demagogue may last only a few minutes or hours. Others, formed by united thought over a period of years may have a life of many centuries. Even though they may seem to cease to exist, they will again recur when conditions are suitable, for quite apart from the original mental impulses, the combined mental action of the group builds a "form" in the inner worlds, as we have seen when discussing the magical images. Each age sows in the inner worlds the seeds that, even if they do not immediately take objective being, will ultimately come to germination and fruition in a later age. And, the esoteric teaching avers, those who originally started the group form will find themselves back in reincarnate life at the period when the results of their former group thinking are becoming objectivised on the physical plane, and they will have to work and possibly suffer under the conditions they themselves originated in the past.

There are four types of emotion which may energise such group-minds: Power, Sex, Herd and Religious emotions. Most of these are interblended in varying proportions in every group-mind, but one is predominant. Now the great religions of the world, with their more or less stereotyped rituals, their common emotion and their long life, have built up very definite group-minds, as have the systems of government which have stood for many centuries, as, for example, the British Monarchy. Chivalric Orders, and initiatory fraternities such as the Masons, the Rosicrucians and many others, all have built up very definite and very powerful group minds in the inner worlds.

The strongest religious group in the Western world is the Christian Church and here we have a closely-knit and vitally charged group-mind going back for nearly two thousand years. But in the case of Christianity we have to deal with much more than the sum total of the mental and emotional activity and aspiration of its members. It may help if we consider our physical body. It consists of myriads of cells, constantly growing, reproducing and disintegrating, but retaining a common relationship the result of which we term our physical body. But each cell has its own psychic life, and the combined cell-life forms the *Nephesch* or Animal Soul of the Qabalists.

Moreover the co-ordinate psychic lives of the many cells form a receptacle or vehicle by means of which the Ego or self may come into contact with the material plane.

So the common group thought, emotion and idealism of all the members of the Christian Church forms a vehicle or body through which and by means of which the head of the Christian religion may come into close contact with all the material world. In theological terms, the Church is the extension of the Incarnation: Just as the psychic health of each cell in the body depends upon its co-ordination with all the others, and just as certain groups of cells are specialised within the general group for special duties, e.g., organs, nerves and sense organs, so in the body which is the Church we find a similar specialisation and functionalism. Entrance into the corporate cell-life of the body is possible by an identification of the psychic life of the individual substance ingested into the system with the common life, and herein, incidentally, is the key to the varying problems of bodily nutrition.

In exactly the same way, the individual becomes part of the group by a similar identification of his psychic self with the common life of the group, and this mental and psychic process is almost invariably accomplished by some rite of admission, such as baptism. Possibly the only exceptions to this are the Society of Friends or Quakers, as they are more commonly known, and the Salvation Army.

Now in the baptismal service the individual is linked mentally with the group mind of the whole Church, and this link is made through the agency of one who is a member of that group and acts by its authority. Even in cases where baptism is performed in emergency by a layman or even a non-Christian, their mental "intention" to link up the newcomer with the group is sufficient. But, it may be objected, in the rite of the Infant Baptism the child cannot consciously identify itself with the Church. Consciously, no, but man is greater than his conscious mind, as we have seen, and the child links itself subconsciously through the officiating minister, with the life of the whole. The godparents should also provide extra links between the child and the Church – though it is very doubtful whether many do that, or even realise they can!

Now what is the result of this piece of initiatory magic? The child is put into the circulation of the Life of the Divine Head of the Church, and the conditions are provided whereby he or she may begin the journey from the chaos of the past, which is built into the subconsciousness, and become *in posse* what they have always been *in esse,* a child of God. So the Anglican Catechism says that baptism is "a death unto sin and a new birth unto righteousness," and this is the formula of all true initiations. Water is used as a symbol of cleansing and is blessed with that intention, using the Christian sign of power, the cross. In the old Mystery religions the initiation was preceded by cleansing lustrations and the waters of baptism are the Christian counterpart of the lustrations of the Mysteries.

Although the child has been initiated into the Christian community, and has begun to partake of the spiritual life thereof, this baptismal initiation is but the earthly shadow of the true Christian initiation of New Birth. The true initiation takes place when the personal self is for a moment caught up to and united with its Greater Self of which it is the earthly expression, and through that Greater Self with the Logos in whom it lives and moves and has its being. So a great mystic, Angelus Silesius has written:

Though Christ a thousand times in Bethlehem be born,
And not within thy heart, thou art left forlorn.
The Cross on Calvary thou lookest to in vain,
Except within thy heart it be set up again.

The experience of "conversion" is an unregulated form of this Christian initiation, hence its importance from the Nonconformist point of view.

To return to the general question of initiatory rites, all true ceremonies link up the neophyte with the life of the group mind and also implant within him the seeds of power which it is hoped will at a future time bring him to a conscious "realisation" of his true nature.

A friend possessing psychic vision made the following report upon an initiatory rite that was worked in his presence:

When the minor Officers in the Lodge made their ceremonial contact with the candidate, his aura became luminous, each portion of the aura corresponding to the particular Office shone brilliantly. Observation of the new member at a later date showed that the effect is relatively permanent – at least in this case.

"When, however, the magus of the lodge made his contact it appeared as if a minute portion of his subtle body was detached from the region of the heart centre; a brilliant minute seed of golden white light seemed to pass down through the aura of the candidate until it came to rest in the region of the solar plexus. Later observation suggests that this is a permanent effect."

A similar, though far more intense phenomena has been recorded by other clairvoyants studying the ordination of a priest in those sections of the Church which have retained the "Apostolic Succession." Perhaps after all, it may fall to the lot of the despised magician to confirm the claims of the Church concerning its priesthood !

In this chapter the Christian baptism has been used as an illustration, but the principles involved are not peculiar to Christianity. The Mystery religions of the Mediterranean basin in the classical period used the same symbolism and very similar rites. In the Mithraic rites the "washing in the Blood of the Lamb (or Bull)" was realistically performed in the "kriobolium" or "taurobolium," where the initiate, robed in white, stood under a grating upon which a lamb or bull was slain, and was thus literally washed in the sacrificial blood. Some of the parallels with Christian symbolism are very close, so much so, in fact, that some of the Christian Fathers explained them by saying that the Devil, knowing what Christianity would be, had guided the heathen to copy what would later be revealed! Others, not Christian apologists have said that this similarity proves that Christianity borrowed its sacramental system from the preceding religions.

The magical tradition avers that the Christian religion, founded on certain principles, expressed itself in similar forms to those of the pagan world around, but redeemed them from the corruption into which they had fallen. It also suggests that the Christian Church had no need to borrow its rites and forms, since it had its roots in the secret tradition of the Hebrews, and what is infinitely more, it was founded and directed by the Supreme Master of all the Mysteries. The "Mysteries of Jesus" of the early Church could hold their own against any of the surrounding Mystery religions. In any case, a religion manifests its vitality in just this assimilation of the best elements in other systems. The Church, like the wise householder of the parable, brings forth from her treasure store things both old and new.

# POSTSCRIPT

*I have written diffusely, leaving many loose ends of thought and this for a very definite reason.*

*There is in the modern world far too much of the "tabloid" spirit – neat little digests of information made up into attractive mental packets for the use of those who wish to have a general knowledge of various subjects, without the trouble of really studying them.*

*Such a thing is highly dangerous, since it offers an ideal way in that the unscrupulous may put forward his or her own particular ideas without any mental resistance on the part of the victim. Such methods lead to the production of the mass mentality that can be such a deadly thing in the hands of the dictators - whether of the Right or the Left.*

*I have, therefore, not produced a "Digest of Magic," but have merely attempted to give my readers some glimpses – intriguing, or even exasperating – of the wonderful field of study which goes by the name of "Magic," and it is my hope that such glimpses will set them studying the works of those who are the recognised masters of the subject.*

# BIBLIOGRAPHY

*The Tree of Life* Israel Regardie (Rider)
*The Mystical Qabalah* Dion Fortune (Williams & Norgate)
*Recovering the Ancient Magic* Max Freedom Long
*In Defence of Magic* Catherine Cook (Rider)
*Egyptian Magic* Dr.Wynn Westcott Out of Print
*Transcendental Magic* Eliphas Levi (Rider)

Other titles available from Thoth Publications

**APPRENTICED TO MAGIC**
*By W.E.Butler*

This volume is for the true aspirant after magical attainment. In his earlier books the author has defined the real magical art and described the training to be undergone by the serious student. Now he goes a step further, and has written a book which, if properly read, meditated upon, and followed up, will bring those who are ready to the doors of the Mysteries.

This book is not for those who seek sensation. It has been written by one who has himself followed the magical path as a sound and competent guide for all who seek initiation into the Western Mysteries.

Contents include:

Application Accepted
First Exercises
Postures and Breathing
Meditation
The Tree of Life
The Tree as an Indicator
The Contact of Power
Bring Through the Power
The Gates are Open

ISBN 978-1-870450-41-6

# HOW TO DEVELOP CLAIRVOYANCE
*By W.E.Butler*

**Everybody's Guide to Supernormal Sense Perception.**

Clairvoyance simply means 'clear seeing'.

In other words, the ability to see things beyond the normal range of our physical sight. It is usually thought of as a gift, granted only to seers, prophets and fortune-tellers.
**Not so. Clairvoyance can be developed – by anyone.** The scrying glass, the crystal ball, the sand disc may seem to belong firmly in the land of fairy tale, but the incredible truth is that, with proper preparation and discipline, they can become reliable tools for bringing psychic perceptions through the subconscious mind into waking consciousness.

This book, by an eminent writer on the occult, gives detailed instructions for developing the power of clear seeing,

**The power is there. It can be tapped – by you.**

ISBN 978-1-870450-46-1

## MAGIC AND THE QABALAH
*By W.E.Butler*

Although the Qabalah may be said to have its origin in some of the earliest experience and speculation of the Hebrew race, it also contains immemorial traditions which have come to us from the Night of Time and from a land now lost. This composite tradition forms the theme of W.E.Butler's stimulating book, in which the noted occultist has sought to illumine as well as to instruct, aiming his writing at the deeper levels of his readers' minds.

The word QBL, from which the name 'Qabalah' is formed, signifies 'from mouth to ear': it was an unwritten tradition of esoteric knowledge passed from one generation to initiates to another in an unbroken line. Although Western scholars question the accuracy of such oral transmissions, W.E.Butler studied them in India and claims they can be very accurate indeed. however, there comes a time when some part of the oral teachings is committed to paper, and it is the accumulation of these writings over the centuries that constitutes the historical Qabalah.

The author promises that those who, having read this book, will use its chapters as food for meditition practice, will find therein something which will be helpful in the work of producing those changes of consciousness which are the goals of magical art. He wishes to pass on to others 'some of the glimpses of reality which it has been my good fortune to have received myself'.

ISBN 978-1-870450-51-5

# HOW TO READ THE AURA
*By W.E.Butler*

Its Character and Function in Everyday Life.

Occult theory states that around all living things is a luminous emanation – the aura.

With practice, the aura can be glimpsed, and this book provides simple but effective techniques for developing auric sight.

With this capability, the occultist can control and re-charge his store of psychic energy, combat psychic vampirism, and diagnose illness in the material body.

Reading the aura is a practical means of living to your full physical and spiritual potential. It is also a revelation of the true nature of man.

In this compelling book, the author explains several ways by which auric sight may be developed, including a method of viewing the aura by direct vision. Techniques of etheric healing are given and the author also explains the colours of the aura, etheric leakage, psychic vampirism and how to re-charge one's etheric 'batteries'.

ISBN 978-1-870450-42-3

# DION FORTUNE AND THE INNER LIGHT
*By Gareth Knight*

At last – a comprehensive biography of Dion Fortune based upon the archives of the Society of the Inner Light. As a result much comes to light that has never before been revealed. This includes:

Her early experiments in trance mediumship with her Golden Dawn teacher Maiya Curtis-Webb and in Glastonbury with Frederick Bligh Bond, famous for his psychic investigations of Glastonbury Abbey.

The circumstances of her first contact with the Masters and reception of "The Cosmic Doctrine". The ambitious plans of the Master of Medicine and the projected esoteric clinic with her husband in the role of Dr. Taverner.

The inside story of the confrontation between the Christian Mystic Lodge of the Theosophical Society of which she was president, and Bishop Piggot of the Liberal Catholic church, over the Star in the East movement and Krishnamurti. Also her group's experience of the magical conflict with Moina MacGregor Mathers.

How she and her husband befriended the young Israel Regardie, were present at his initiation into the Hermes Temple of the Stella Matutina, and suffered a second ejection from the Golden Dawn on his subsequent falling out with it.

Her renewed and highly secret contact with her old Golden Dawn teacher Maiya Tranchell-Hayes and their development of the esoteric side of the Arthurian legends.

Her peculiar and hitherto unknown work in policing the occult jurisdiction of the Master for whom she worked which brought her into unlikely contact with occultists such as Aleister Crowley.

Nor does the remarkable story end with her physical death for, through the mediumship of Margaret Lumley Brown and others, continued contacts with Dion Fortune have been reported over subsequent years.

ISBN 978-1-870450-45-4

# AN INTRODUCTION TO RITUAL MAGIC
*By Dion Fortune & Gareth Knight*

At the time this was something of a unique event in esoteric publishing – a new book by the legendary Dion Fortune. Especially with its teachings on the theory and practice of ritual or ceremonial magic, by one who, like the heroine of two of her other novels, was undoubtedly "a mistress of that art".

In this work Dion Fortune deals in successive chapters with Types of Mind Working; Mind Training; The Use of Ritual; Psychic Perception; Ritual Initiation; The Reality of the Subtle Planes; Focusing the Magic Mirror; Channelling the Forces; The Form of the Ceremony; and The Purpose of Magic - with appendices on Talisman Magic and Astral Forms.

Each chapter is supplemented and expanded by a companion chapter on the same subject by Gareth Knight. In Dion Fortune's day the conventions of occult secrecy prevented her from being too explicit on the practical details of magic, except in works of fiction. These veils of secrecy having now been drawn back, Gareth Knight has taken the opportunity to fill in much practical information that Dion Fortune might well have included had she been writing today.

In short, in this unique collaboration of two magical practitioners and teachers, we are presented with a valuable and up-to-date text on the practice of ritual or ceremonial magic "as it is". That is to say, as a practical, spiritual, and psychic discipline, far removed from the lurid superstition and speculation that are the hall mark of its treatment in sensational journalism and channels of popular entertainment.

ISBN 978-1-870450 26 3

## THE PATH THROUGH THE LABYRINTH
*by Marian Green*

The Quest for Initiation into the Western Mystery Tradition.

Underlying the evolving culture of the West there hides a complete strata of folk-lore, of traditional skills and wisdom, of ancient arts and festivals.

These are still emerging in myth and legend, in song and celebrations, each retaining aspects of a very great initiatory system rooted in the land and its magic.

Most available sources tell the reader about the how to of magic, but for the first time this book explores the way of magic, and the what happens when... of modern magical techniques.

In *The Path Through the Labyrinth*, Marian Green, a highly respected practitioner and teacher of the Western Tradition, examines these questions and guides the reader safely to the heart of the magical maze, and then out again.

ISBN 978-1-870450-15-7

## PRACTICAL TECHNIQUES OF MODERN MAGIC
*by Marian Green*

What is the essence of ritual magic?
How are the symbols used to create change?
Can I safely take steps in ritual on my own?
How does magic fit into the pattern of life in the modern world?
Will I be able to master the basic arts?

All these questions and many more are answered within the pages of this book.

ISBN 978-1-870450-14-0

www.ingramcontent.com/pod-product-compliance
Lightning Source LLC
Chambersburg PA
CBHW030516100426
42813CB00001B/63

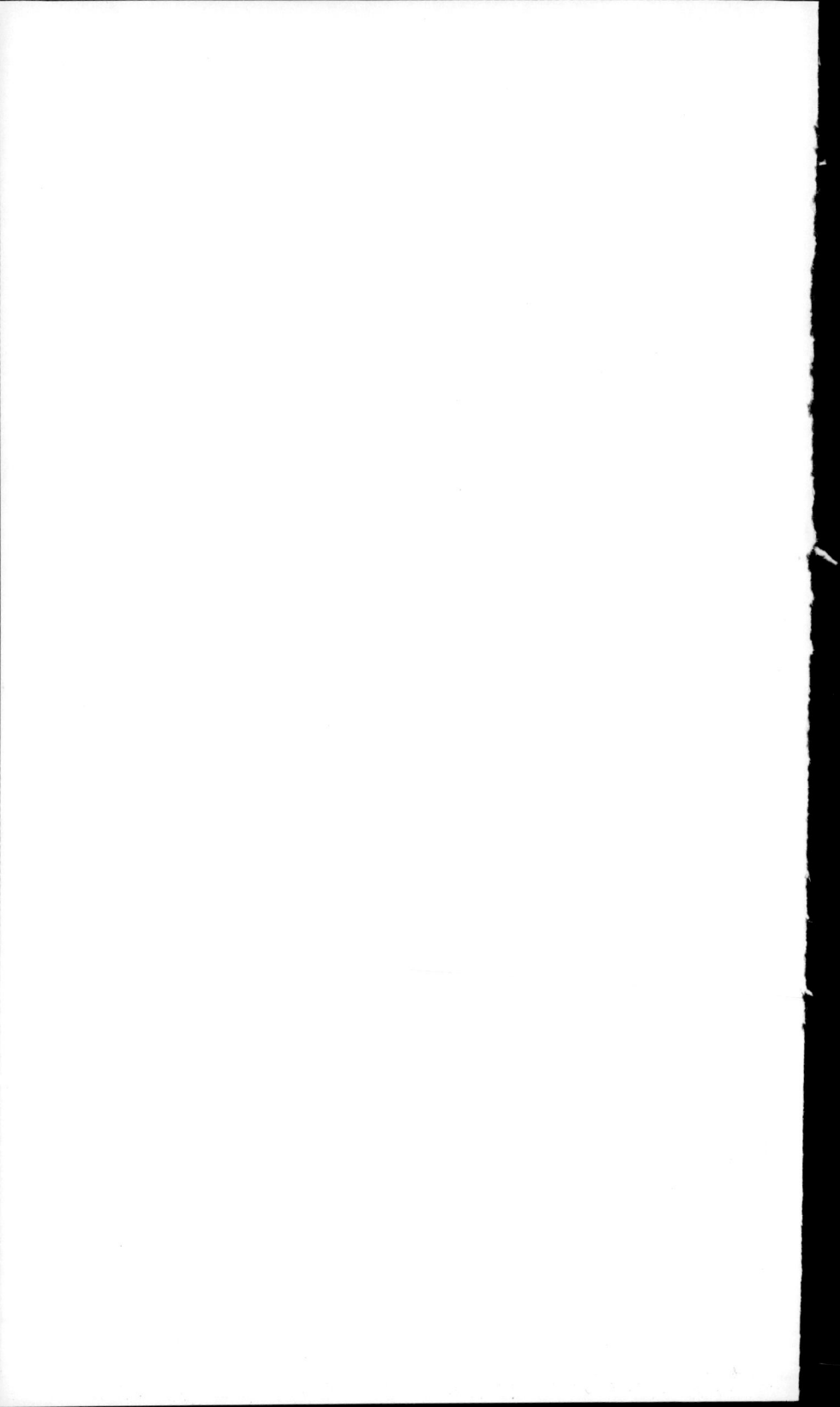